07/06

CONSTRUCTION ZONE

photographs by **Richard Sobol**   text by **Cheryl Willis Hudson**

CANDLEWICK PRESS
CAMBRIDGE, MASSACHUSETTS

What do you see at the construction zone?

The **construction zone** is like a giant puzzle.

Some pieces are very big.

Other pieces are very small.

? _A construction zone is a special area set aside for building._

Before building can begin . . .

the **architect** makes lots
of drawings and models.
These show how the
finished building will look.

Everyone at the construction zone
will follow the architect's plan.

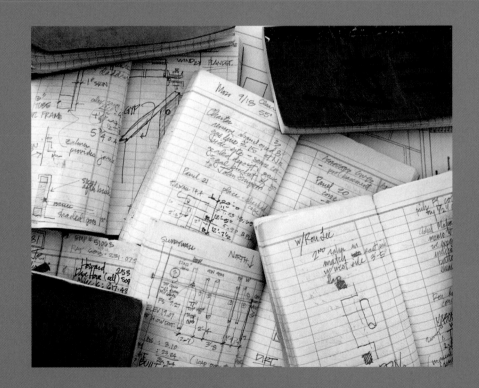

 *An architect is someone who designs buildings
and makes sure that they are built properly.*

The amazing work begins. . . .

Big yellow machines dig their claws
deep into the ground.

They **excavate** the site and move mounds and mounds of soil and stone.

To excavate means to dig in the earth.

There are lots of workers at the construction zone.
They wear **hard hats**, heavy gloves, goggles,
and steel-tipped shoes to protect their bodies.
Construction work can be dirty and dangerous.

 Hard hats must be worn by construction workers on the job to protect their heads from falling objects.

A temporary wall is put into the ground to keep the dirt
from sliding back into the excavated hole.

Now the foundation is laid.
This is what the building will sit on.

Starting from the bottom,
ironworkers lay down a mesh of **rebar**.

They tie the long rods tight!

 *Rebar is a building material made from steel and
used inside concrete forms to make them stronger.*

Watch your step!

Day after day, **concrete** spews from the
mixing trucks parked along the street.

It squishes and slides between the iron rods.
The concrete dries into smooth stonelike slabs.

 *Concrete is a building material made from
a mixture of sand, gravel, cement, and water.*

Men and women work together at
the construction zone.

They use smart minds and strong muscles
to make every piece of the puzzle fit.

Big hooks and **cranes** hoist steel beams up.
Careful now!

The workers gently guide the heavy **beams** and fasten them into place to make the building **frame**.

A crane is a machine with a long arm used to lift and move heavy objects. The steel beam frame is like a skeleton that gives the building shape.

Carpenters saw and hammer and drill and sand.
They make hollow wooden forms in the
shapes of floors and **columns**.
Then concrete is poured inside of them.
When it dries, the wood is removed.

The columns and floors are put into place.

These concrete slabs look like a stack of pancakes!

 A carpenter is someone who works with wood or builds and repairs the wooden parts of a building. A column is a tall pillar that helps separate and support the floors of a building.

High above the ground, construction workers balance on planks and beams like circus tightrope walkers.

There are no stairs or elevators yet, so they move around on **scaffolds**. The workers must wear **harnesses** to keep them safe.

Masons begin to lay brick after brick, higher and higher.
The outside walls go up!

 A scaffold is a structure of wooden planks, ropes, and metal poles that workers stand on high above ground. A harness of straps attached to something sturdy catches workers in case they fall.

Next, the construction workers
install the **insulation** and windows.

Steady now!

Piece by piece, the giant orange cranes
move the windows into place.
These huge panes of glass let sunlight in but
keep wind and moisture out.

 Insulation is a special material that stops heat from escaping through the walls.
It helps keep the building warmer in winter and cooler in summer.

Between the walls and under the floors,
miles and miles of **cables** and **cords** and
wires, and **pipes** and **vents** are laid.

The building must have power,
water, heat, and air conditioning for
the people who will work inside.

 Cables, cords, and wires are used for carrying electricity and television and telephone signals. Pipes carry running water for sinks and toilets, and vents allow fresh air in and send stale air out.

Inside, the walls are painted,
fixtures installed, cabinets built,
carpets laid, and furniture arranged.

Finally, a place to sit!

It is a comfortable place to think
and talk and share ideas.

 Fixtures are items that are put firmly and permanently in place, such as doorknobs, faucets, and lighting.

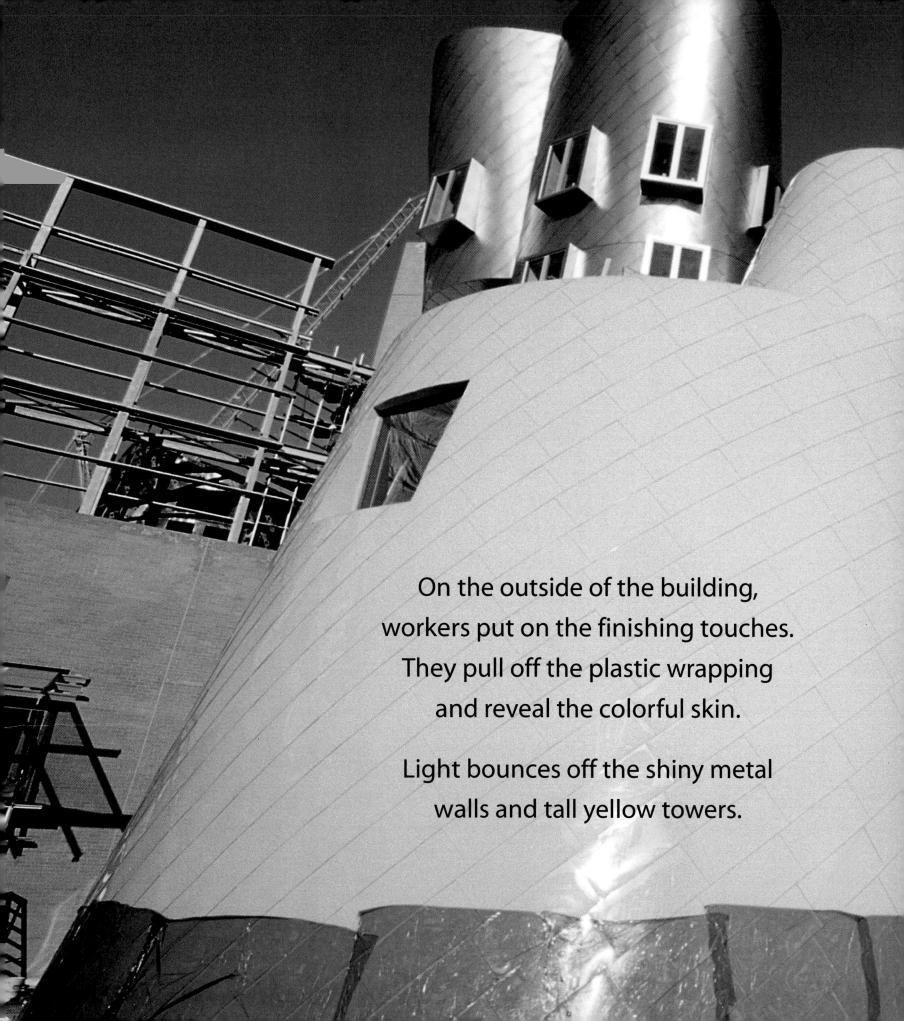

On the outside of the building,
workers put on the finishing touches.
They pull off the plastic wrapping
and reveal the colorful skin.

Light bounces off the shiny metal
walls and tall yellow towers.

Nighttime falls at the construction zone.

It is quiet and still.

Inside the building, lights are shining.

Outside, trees have been planted on a rooftop.

The pieces of a giant puzzle have finally fit into place.

The photographs in this book were made over a three-year period at the building site of Massachusetts Institute of Technology's Stata Center in Cambridge, Massachusetts, designed by celebrated architect Frank O. Gehry. At the start of excavation in January 2001, I was given a walk-through by the safety superintendent. Sensing that I was new to this world, he pointed out some of the dangers of the process around me — holes that I could disappear through or concrete pools that I could drown in. He was concerned that while I was peering forward to take a picture, a load of steel might whack me from behind. After hearing this, I was glad to have someone who knew more than I did about construction sites follow me around.

While I photographed, I was continually amazed by the construction workers, who faced many challenges in bringing to life a building with so many sharp angles and a mixture of materials, including brick, steel, and glass. This was a large project, yet it was built by placing one wire here and installing one drain pipe there, lowering one beam here and fitting in one door there — each action repeated by dozens of people working together to solve a great puzzle.

However, the images of a construction zone evaporate through time: the vast majority of the work, despite its beauty, craftsmanship, and detail, will disappear behind a wall of Sheetrock or a slab of concrete or a layer of waterproofing material. These photographs are a record of a few moments from the construction process — isolated, unique, and often surprising — much like the finished project itself.

Richard Sobol

For everyone in the world except Dave Lewis
R. S.

To the staff and children of
the Jersey Explorer Children's Museum —
keep on building
C. W. H.

Text copyright © 2006 by Cheryl Willis Hudson
Photographs copyright © 2006 by Richard Sobol
Endpaper images used by permission of Gehry Partners, LLP
Some of the photographs in this book were previously published in *Building Stata: The Design and Construction
of Frank O. Gehry's Stata Center at MIT* (MIT Press, 2004).

First edition 2006

Library of Congress Cataloging-in-Publication Data

Hudson, Cheryl Willis.
Construction zone / photographs by Richard Sobol ; text by Cheryl Willis Hudson. — 1st ed.
p.   cm
ISBN 0-7636-2684-8
1. Building Sites — Juvenile literature. 2. Building — Juvenile literature. I. Title
TH375.H83 2006
690 — dc22   2005050793

2 4 6 8 10 9 7 5 3 1

Printed in China

This book was typeset in Myriad.

Candlewick Press
2067 Massachusetts Avenue
Cambridge, Massachusetts 02140

visit us at www.candlewick.com